STERLING CHILDREN'S BOOKS
New York

An Imprint of Sterling Publishing Co., Inc.
1166 Avenue of the Americas
New York, NY 10036

ISBN 978-1-4549-3870-5

Distributed in Canada by Sterling Publishing Co., Inc.
c/o Canadian Manda Group, 664 Annette Street
Toronto, Ontario M6S 2C8, Canada

For information about custom editions, special sales, and premium and corporate
purchases, please contact Sterling Special Sales at 800-805-5489 or specialsales@
sterlingpublishing.com.

Manufactured in China

Lot #:
10 9 8 7 6 5 4 3 2 1
07/19

sterlingpublishing.com

Translation: Langue & Parole, Milan (Karen Tomatis)

SUPERHEROES WITHOUT CAPES

Discover the Super Powers of 20 Famous People,
and Find Your Own, Too!

Written by Federica Magrin

Illustrations by Isabella Grott

STERLING CHILDREN'S BOOKS
New York

Coco Chanel

Anne Frank

Mahatma Gandhi

Frida Kahlo

Albert Einstein

Malala Yousafzai

Nelson Mandela

Marie Curie

Stephen Hawking

Contents

Introduction

What is a superhero? A person with uncommon powers? Someone who has a special mission to carry out, like saving humanity?

Reading the pages of this book you will discover that HISTORY, especially recent history, IS FULL OF MEN AND WOMEN WHO POSSESSED GREAT TALENTS and who committed themselves to making sure Earth continued to be a beautiful place to live in.

There's FRIDA with her great passion for art, the brilliant EINSTEIN with his sardonic smile, courageous GANDHI with his patience and nonviolence, the adventurous ARMSTRONG and his first leaps on the moon's surface...

TWENTY PEOPLE, MEN AND WOMEN, tell you about their successes, the incredible results they achieved, and their victories, but also their fears and their uncertainties. Men and women like you, with generous hearts, who were not perfect, but certainly filled with good intentions.

Are you ready to listen to their stories and retrace their steps?
A UNIQUE VOYAGE WITH SUPER PEOPLE IN THEIR EVERY DAY LIVES AWAITS YOU.

Emmeline Pankhurst 1858–1928

Never underestimate the power we women HAVE TO DEFINE OUR OWN DESTINIES. I think I repeated this sentence to myself all my life as an encouragement. When you are born into a male-dominated society, you have only two options: conform to the system; take care of your husband, children, and the domestic chores, as everyone thinks you should; or fight to become a citizen of your country just as any man. I was born in England in a family where politics were considered very important, and I had the good fortune to marry a man, Richard Pankhurst, who, like me, believed WOMEN SHOULD HAVE THE RIGHT TO VOTE. I shaped my own destiny, and I used every means to reach my goal: equal rights for men and women. I succeeded up to a certain point. Do you know how? With my super power: PERSISTENCE.

My political battle for WOMEN'S RIGHT TO VOTE meant
that I was not well loved, and even today there are those
who, together with praises for my work, cast doubts on my
person. I was certainly extreme and not inclined to give
up on what I believed was the foundation of my political
action. I don't deny having had doubts, especially regarding
my daughters' participation in the movement, but I never
for one moment stopped thinking that I WAS DOING THE
RIGHT THING, not only for myself, but FOR FUTURE
GENERATIONS. Just a few weeks before my death, the
right to vote in England was given to women over 21 years
of age. It was a historical event, and I am proud to have
contributed toward it, but it was just the beginning of a
battle that others would fight across the world – a battle
that continues even today. Don't ever give up!

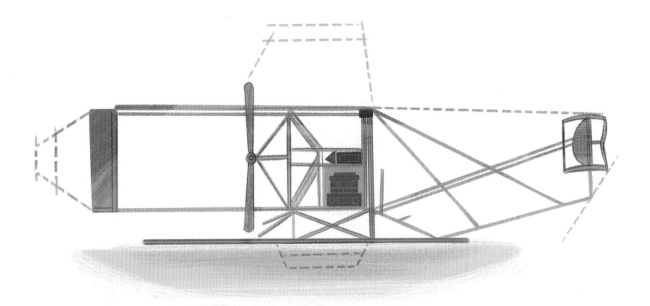

the Wright Brothers

WILBUR 1867–1912 AND ORVILLE 1871–1948

TO BE ABLE TO FLY IS A DREAM as ancient as mankind: the myth of Icarus, who flew to the sun with wings made of wax, Leonardo da Vinci's flying machines projects. . . . But we didn't only want to imagine flight, we actually wanted to make it happen. Since our childhood we were lively, creative children who loved to fantasize and study the whys and hows of things. Mechanics was definitely our thing. We dedicated ourselves to printing, then to bicycles, but it was the prospect of creating a flying machine that infused passion into our lives. We turned to our SUPER POWER, OUR VISIONARY MIND, and we began planning our flying machine, the *Flyer* and. . . we flew!

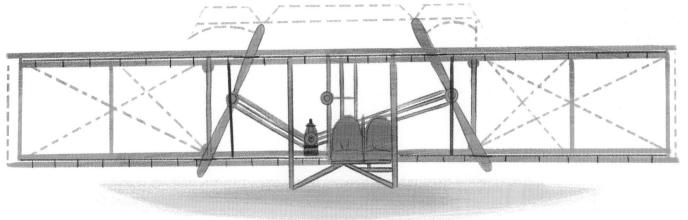

Others had tried to fly a motorized vehicle that was heavier than air, but they had failed. That is why, when we heard the news that Samuel Langley, a brilliant inventor, had failed, we knew it was our turn, but what were our chances? Nevertheless, we made it, and WE FLEW A STABLE 118 FT (36 METER) FLIGHT THAT LASTED 12 SECONDS. Even if it was only a small leap forward, that first flight WAS A HISTORIC EVENT FOR MANKIND. It was December 17, 1903 and the world would never be the same again. This event marked the beginning of AN EXTRAORDINARY ERA in which men would conquer the air that, until then, had been the exclusive domain of birds. It was a fantastic experience that remained in our minds forever. *More than anything else, the sensation [of flying] is one of perfect peace mingled with an excitement that strains every nerve to the utmost.*

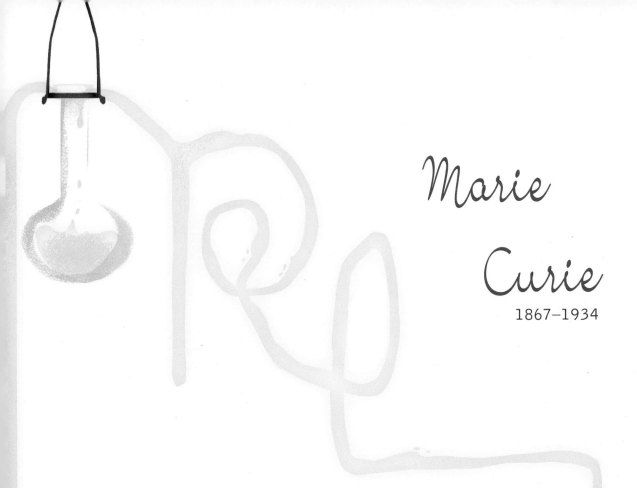

Marie Curie

1867–1934

When I was born, in Poland, and around the world in general, women did not have many options. We could take on a few jobs, but we were mostly seen as housewives and mothers, certainly not as individuals who could choose a career in anything she liked. Only men could do that. But I WANTED TO DEVOTE MY LIFE TO SCIENCE, work in a laboratory, and further my knowledge in physics and chemistry. I am known as MARIE CURIE, but Curie was my husband's name. I was born Marie Skłodowska, and I was THE FIRST WOMAN to teach at the Sorbonne University, THE FIRST TO BE AWARDED TWO NOBEL PRIZES for physics and chemistry, and the first to have two chemical elements named after her. My super power was DETERMINATION: I used it until the very end, to carry out my research in the interest of humanity, because *I was taught that the way of progress is neither swift nor easy.*

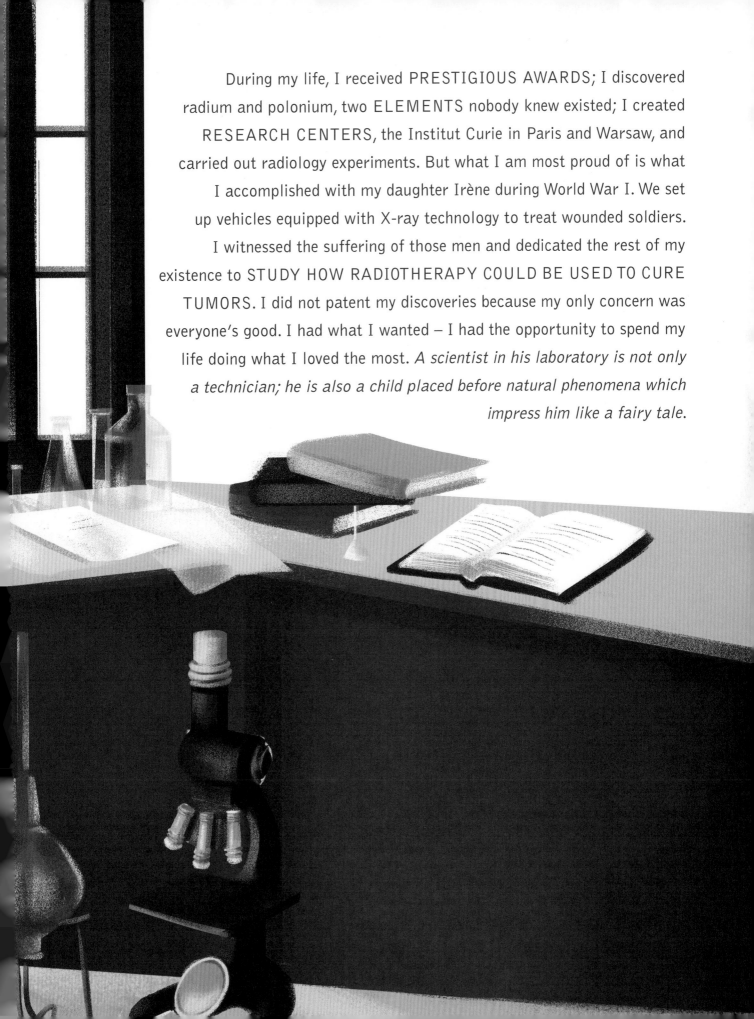

During my life, I received PRESTIGIOUS AWARDS; I discovered radium and polonium, two ELEMENTS nobody knew existed; I created RESEARCH CENTERS, the Institut Curie in Paris and Warsaw, and carried out radiology experiments. But what I am most proud of is what I accomplished with my daughter Irène during World War I. We set up vehicles equipped with X-ray technology to treat wounded soldiers. I witnessed the suffering of those men and dedicated the rest of my existence to STUDY HOW RADIOTHERAPY COULD BE USED TO CURE TUMORS. I did not patent my discoveries because my only concern was everyone's good. I had what I wanted – I had the opportunity to spend my life doing what I loved the most. *A scientist in his laboratory is not only a technician; he is also a child placed before natural phenomena which impress him like a fairy tale.*

Mahatma Gandhi
1869–1948

They called me "Mahatma," THE GREAT
SOUL, but I never liked that name because
I NEVER BELIEVED THAT GREAT AND
SMALL SOULS COULD EXIST.
My real name was Mohandas Karamchand Gandhi.
I was born into a wealthy and influential Indian family,
and as a young man, I wasn't a champion for the rights
of my people. I went to London to study law, and I lived
as a Westerner. After earning my degree, I returned to
India and started my work as a lawyer. I went to South
Africa to follow a work lawsuit, and that is where
I realized that the Indians who worked there were heavily
discriminated against. I could not turn my head away from
the situation. That was when my battle began – a battle that
I believed had to be fought with my SUPER POWER:
NONVIOLENCE.

Today on the Indian flag you see a CHARKHA, a wheel for spinning cotton. It is the symbol of one of my victories, the boycott of textiles from other countries. It also represents the REBIRTH OF MY COUNTRY, India, that for too long had been subjected to foreign rule. A deep sense of justice and equality made me become a leader, but an equally deep sense of brotherhood induced me to use the weapon of passive RESISTANCE, REJECTING VIOLENCE. I carried on with my battle, enduring the hardships of prison and fasting. During my most famous march, I walked for twenty-four days to the Indian Ocean to collect salt and show how wrong and oppressive the tax on this essential commodity was.

By living a life of integrity, I wanted to live by this principle: *BE THE CHANGE THAT YOU WANT TO SEE IN THE WORLD.*

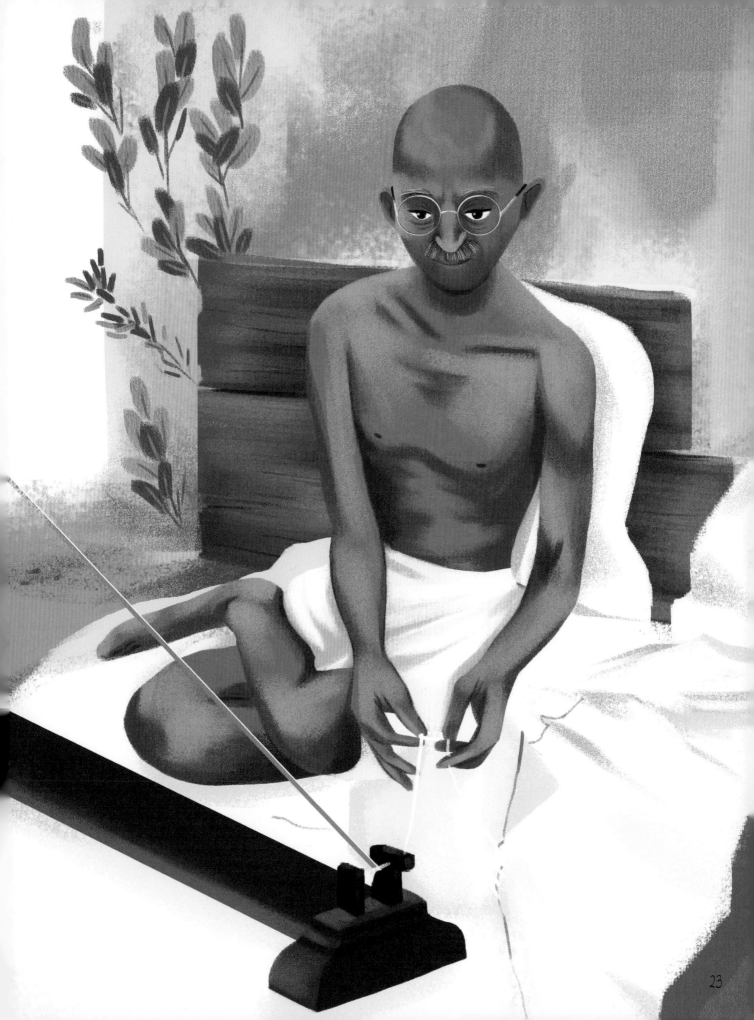

Albert Einstein 1879–1955

They said I was a genius, but I was not. I was A NORMAL PERSON, but I was
also VERY CURIOUS. I loved mathematics and physics, two subjects
that are often considered to be difficult. But if you think about my most famous
formula, $E=mc^2$, it doesn't look that complicated, does it? It's an equation that
explains how the energy of a celestial body equals its mass times the speed
of light squared. Well okay, perhaps it's not that simple, but this equation told
us how to transform mass into energy and vice versa, a discovery that turned
out to be quite a breakthrough in science. So if I ever did have the GENIUS
SUPER POWER, it was only BECAUSE I WAS GIVEN THE OPPORTUNITY
TO STUDY WHAT I LIKED: *Everybody is a genius. But if you judge a fish by
its ability to climb a tree, it will live its whole life believing that it is stupid.*

I was awarded a Nobel Prize for Physics, I taught at a
university, I held lectures in the most prestigious universities
all over the world, and when I died, they studied my brain
to understand what made it so special. But that's not where
MY GENIUS CAME FROM — my genius stemmed from my
INEXHAUSTIBLE PASSION FOR DISCOVERY and my
desire to understand the deepest causes of all things around
us. I didn't always get the results I hoped for, and
I was often labeled as a lazy person, especially when I was
young. I used to study only the subjects that I liked, and
I didn't pay too much attention to what people told me.
Besides my thirst for knowledge, I always stayed true to my
critical sensibility and to a deep sense of justice that urged
me to fight for peace and equality. The photo that represents
me the most is the one where I am sticking my tongue out,
because it shows that even when WE GROW UP, WE MUST
ALWAYS KEEP THE CHILD INSIDE US ALIVE!

Coco Chanel

1883–1971

Everybody knows me as
COCO CHANEL, a name that
today is synonymous with FASHION, TASTE, AND ELEGANCE.
But few know that I was born Gabrielle Bonheur Chanel, one of
the many children of a poor family living in the town of Saumur
in France. When I was young, I was abandoned in an orphanage.
That was where I learned to sew and to make an art out of the
simple work of a seamstress. With a rather special super power,
SELF-DETERMINATION, I decided that once
I left the orphanage, I would be the owner of
my life and that being a woman would not
get in the way of me reaching the
goals I had set myself.
My FEMININITY, I
RESOLVED, WOULD
BE MY STRENGTH.
In fact, I always
believed that
*in order to be
irreplaceable, one
must always be
different*. The fact
that what I created has
outlived me proves that
I was right.

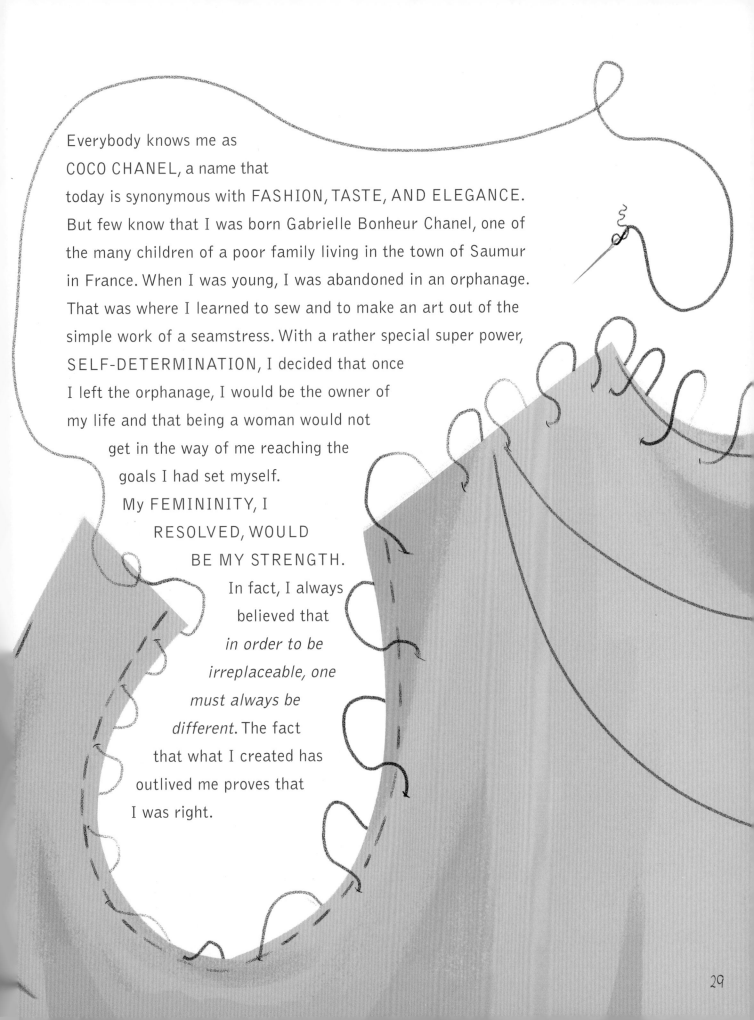

It all started with a HAT collection. We were in the EARLY 1900s, the world was racing toward progress (cars, trains, planes, electricity, etc.) while women were still wearing stiff, redundant, and scarcely functional clothing. And so, looking at them move, sometimes rather clumsily, I thought that the moment had come for WOMEN TO START EXPERIMENTING, to live more freely in their bodies, feeling they were the protagonists of their lives, without losing any of their elegance and femininity. I began to create CLOTHES that WOULD SUIT A NEW KIND OF WOMAN – a woman who worked and operated in the world just like a man. I designed functional suits, outfits that enhanced the figure without being vulgar, and ensembles that allowed women to move comfortably and with elegance. I had highs and lows. My work was celebrated and criticized, and I was praised and despised, but *I regret nothing of my life except that which I did not do.*

Amelia Earhart 1897–1937

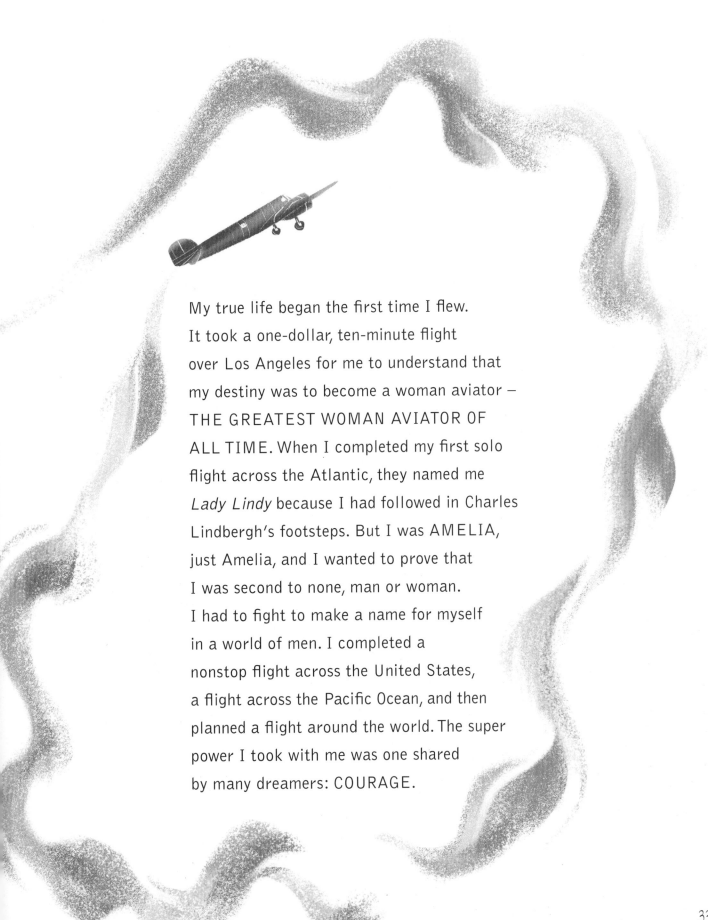

My true life began the first time I flew.
It took a one-dollar, ten-minute flight
over Los Angeles for me to understand that
my destiny was to become a woman aviator –
THE GREATEST WOMAN AVIATOR OF
ALL TIME. When I completed my first solo
flight across the Atlantic, they named me
Lady Lindy because I had followed in Charles
Lindbergh's footsteps. But I was AMELIA,
just Amelia, and I wanted to prove that
I was second to none, man or woman.
I had to fight to make a name for myself
in a world of men. I completed a
nonstop flight across the United States,
a flight across the Pacific Ocean, and then
planned a flight around the world. The super
power I took with me was one shared
by many dreamers: COURAGE.

What I wanted to do was daring, and many people thought I did not have what it takes. But in my opinion, you need to be a bit wild to BELIEVE IN YOUR DREAMS, and YOU MUST FIGHT TO MAKE THEM COME TRUE. My dream was about a 29,000 mile (47,000 km) flight around the world — that would have been a unique endeavor.

When I took off, I could feel my heart pounding: it was really happening!
I was 7,000 miles (11,000 km) from the finish, flying over the Pacific, when something
went wrong.

There were communication problems, not enough fuel, low visibility, and I was flying over
an area with countless small islands. I disappeared with my airplane, the *Electa*, and
Fred Noonan, the navigator who had led me all the way there. Did I fail? Yes and no.
I did not complete my mission, that is a fact, but I OPENED THE WAY for many women
who came after me. I believe that women, like men, should try to do the impossible.
And when they fail, their failure should be a challenge to others.

Frida Kahlo

1907–1954

My full name is long and sounds almost like a tongue twister, but for everyone I have always been FRIDA. During my life I had to resort to many super powers, but the one that most represented me was PASSION.

I think I inherited it from my country, Mexico, where people always trust their hearts. When I was eighteen and it seemed as if my life had been mapped out – I was in love and I was going to university studying to become a doctor – AN ACCIDENT changed my whole destiny. I could have given up everything, let my body decide for me, but instead I FOUGHT WITH THE STRENGTH OF A LION, and I became one of the greatest artists in the world.

When a tram crashed into the bus I was traveling on September 17, 1925, I literally fell to pieces. My back was broken in three places, my pelvis was crushed, and my leg was mangled. When I was discharged from the hospital, I remained bedridden for years, and that is where the REVELATION happened. With the help of a huge mirror fixed to the canopy of my bed, I began to paint SELF-PORTRAITS that told my story, my suffering, my emotions, and my love for life that I discovered in the folds of immense pain. Art allowed me to meet my other GREAT LOVE, DIEGO RIVERA, who was my soul mate until I breathed my last breath. I didn't simply survive through art, I told the story of the PASSION with which I DEVOURED LIFE, despite everything. I can summarize my life in this way: *I'm not ill. I am broken, but I am happy as long as I can paint.*

Mother Teresa of Calcutta 1910–1997

You know me as MOTHER TERESA OF CALCUTTA, but
my real name was Aniezë Gonxhe Bojaxhiu, and I was born
in Skopje, then part of Albania. I was still very young when
I realized my destiny would be in India. At the time, I did not
imagine that my mission would be to devote my life to the
poor, but on the night of August 10, 1946, I had a revelation:
I had to leave the safe haven of the convent and devote my
life to the people suffering a life of misery and pain.
It was not easy. I had to convince my superiors of the value
of my choice, I had to attend a course to learn how to take
care of the sick, and I had to live in a hut in the *Motijhil*
slum in Calcutta among the outcasts and their desperation.
I could only rely on my SUPER POWER – FAITH – but
I was able to convince others to follow my example.
In 1950, I founded my own congregation, the
Missionaries of Charity, with one single mission:
to love others.

When I decided that I would devote my existence to those who had nothing, not even dignity, I took off my black veil and put on a SARI, the simplest and cheapest one, to be NO DIFFERENT FROM ANY OTHER INDIAN WOMAN. I even became a citizen of the country where I chose to serve, and I immersed myself in Calcutta's poorest areas, the SLUMS. I brought comfort to the afflicted, and I took care of the sick, all of them, even the lepers and those who had absolutely nothing. I did not do it to receive recognition, or to become famous, but only because I always thought that even if *we ourselves feel that what we are doing is just a drop in the ocean [...] the ocean would be less because of that missing drop.* I always considered myself *A PENCIL IN GOD'S HANDS*: a tool for a greater good.

Rosa
Parks

1913–2005

I was tired. Not only because it had been a long day at work (I worked as a seamstress), but because I was no longer WILLING TO TAKE THE CONTINUOUS OFFENSE of being considered inferior to others only because of THE COLOR OF MY SKIN. It was December 1, 1955, and I got on the bus as usual. There was only one free seat, and I sat down. The driver told me to get up because that seat was for white people, but I refused. That was why I was arrested. I said NO to something I felt WAS PROFOUNDLY UNFAIR, but I could not imagine that this would prompt the African-American community of Montgomery, Alabama, the city where I lived, to organize the Bus Boycott. I became a hero, A SYMBOL OF SELF-DETERMINATION, but I was only a woman whose super power was her RESOLVE.

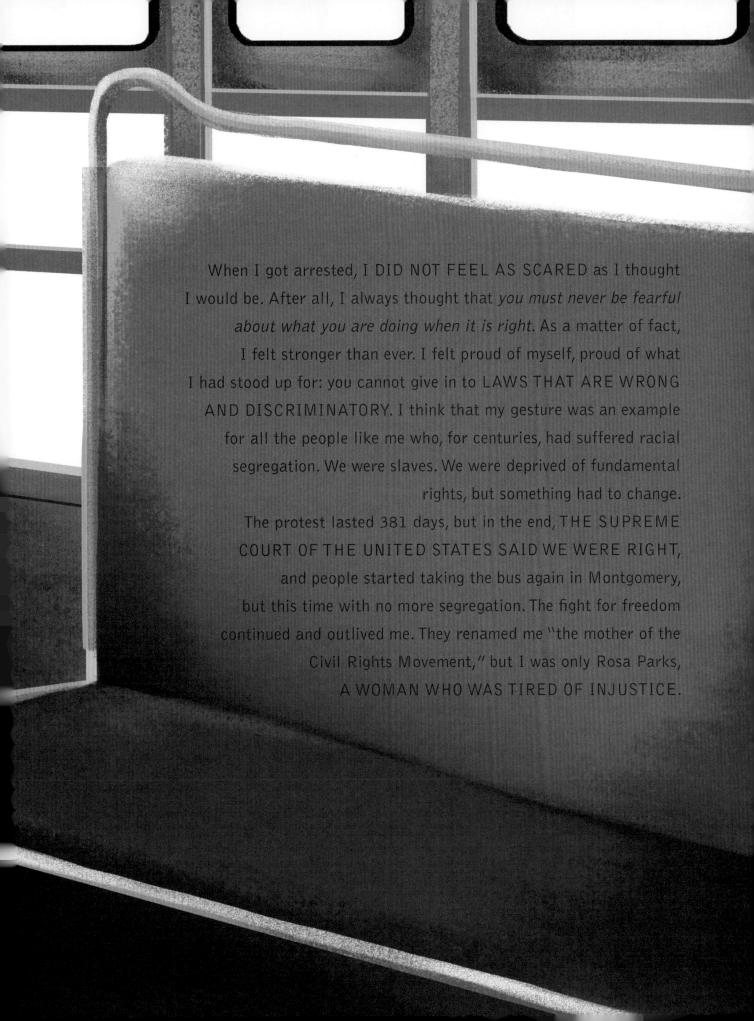

When I got arrested, I DID NOT FEEL AS SCARED as I thought I would be. After all, I always thought that *you must never be fearful about what you are doing when it is right.* As a matter of fact, I felt stronger than ever. I felt proud of myself, proud of what I had stood up for: you cannot give in to LAWS THAT ARE WRONG AND DISCRIMINATORY. I think that my gesture was an example for all the people like me who, for centuries, had suffered racial segregation. We were slaves. We were deprived of fundamental rights, but something had to change.

The protest lasted 381 days, but in the end, THE SUPREME COURT OF THE UNITED STATES SAID WE WERE RIGHT, and people started taking the bus again in Montgomery, but this time with no more segregation. The fight for freedom continued and outlived me. They renamed me "the mother of the Civil Rights Movement," but I was only Rosa Parks, A WOMAN WHO WAS TIRED OF INJUSTICE.

Nelson Mandela
1918–2013

I have often been called *Madiba*, a title that, in my ethnic group, is given only to the greatest of men, but I believe that the name given to me at my birth, Rolihlahla, describes me better. It means "PERSON WHO CAUSES TROUBLE," and I have caused a lot of trouble following my DREAM OF LIBERTY. I was born in South Africa, a country split in two by apartheid, the racial segregation between white people and people of color, and I decided when I was just a boy that I would not leave a world divided in this way as a legacy to my children. In my fight I resorted to every super power I possessed, but above all I relied on PATIENCE. It took 26 years in prison, and a fearless struggle, to achieve what I wanted, but in the end I was able to close my eyes on a LAND THAT HAD FINALLY BECOME UNITED ONCE MORE.

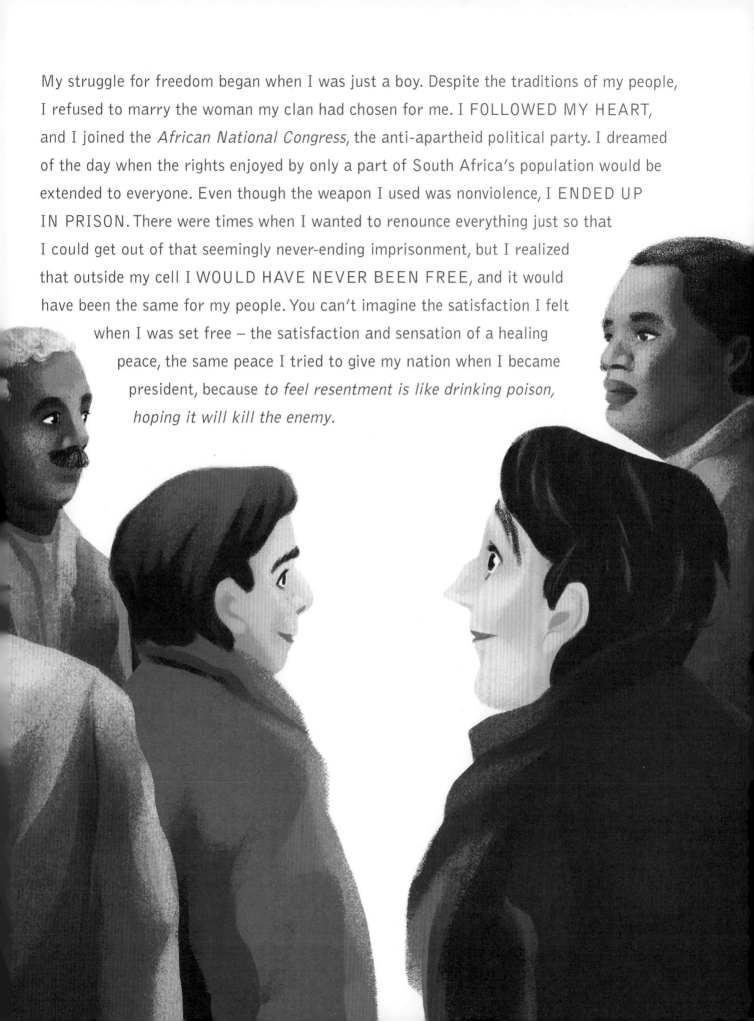

My struggle for freedom began when I was just a boy. Despite the traditions of my people, I refused to marry the woman my clan had chosen for me. I FOLLOWED MY HEART, and I joined the *African National Congress*, the anti-apartheid political party. I dreamed of the day when the rights enjoyed by only a part of South Africa's population would be extended to everyone. Even though the weapon I used was nonviolence, I ENDED UP IN PRISON. There were times when I wanted to renounce everything just so that I could get out of that seemingly never-ending imprisonment, but I realized that outside my cell I WOULD HAVE NEVER BEEN FREE, and it would have been the same for my people. You can't imagine the satisfaction I felt when I was set free – the satisfaction and sensation of a healing peace, the same peace I tried to give my nation when I became president, because *to feel resentment is like drinking poison, hoping it will kill the enemy*.

Anne Frank
1929–1945

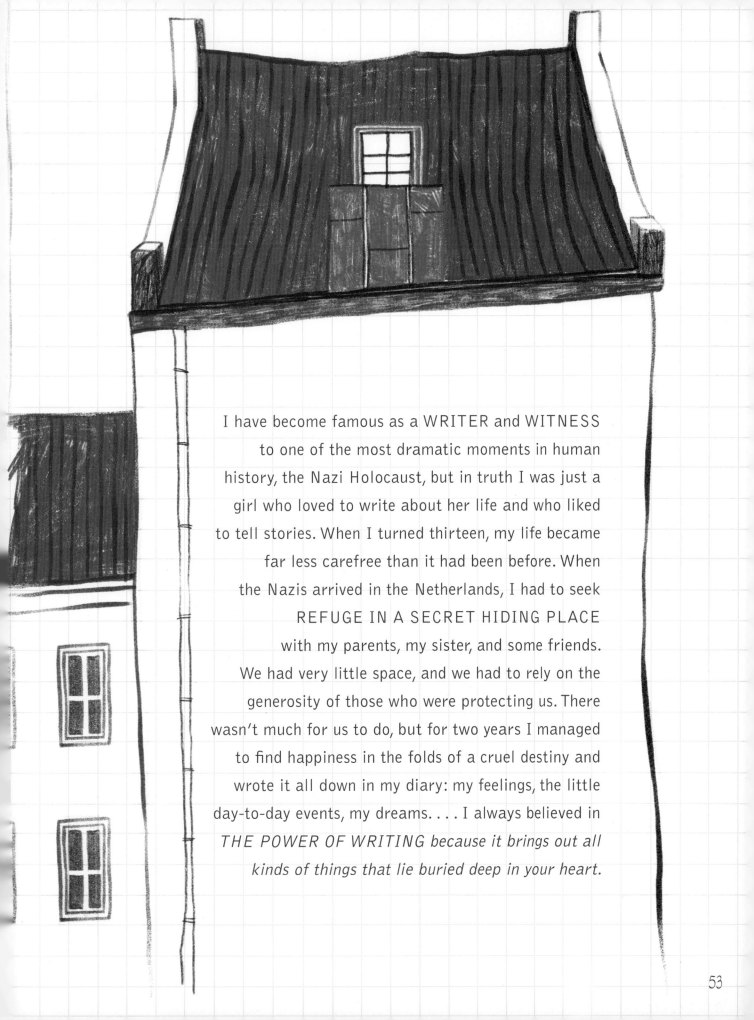

I have become famous as a WRITER and WITNESS
to one of the most dramatic moments in human
history, the Nazi Holocaust, but in truth I was just a
girl who loved to write about her life and who liked
to tell stories. When I turned thirteen, my life became
far less carefree than it had been before. When
the Nazis arrived in the Netherlands, I had to seek
REFUGE IN A SECRET HIDING PLACE
with my parents, my sister, and some friends.
We had very little space, and we had to rely on the
generosity of those who were protecting us. There
wasn't much for us to do, but for two years I managed
to find happiness in the folds of a cruel destiny and
wrote it all down in my diary: my feelings, the little
day-to-day events, my dreams. . . . I always believed in
*THE POWER OF WRITING because it brings out all
kinds of things that lie buried deep in your heart.*

If you could see the BACKHOUSE, our secret hiding place at 263 Prinsengracht, Amsterdam, which today has been turned into a commemorative museum, you would never believe that my family and four other people could LIVE THERE FOR TWO YEARS. It was hard. We couldn't have any contact with others, we couldn't put a scarf on and go out running along the canals like we used to, or go to the flower market, or buy a hot caramel *stroopwafer*. But I made sure they could not take MY DEEPEST FREEDOM from me, the freedom to proclaim my JOY FOR LIFE ITSELF, to write my opinions, to feel love, and to look up to the sky. Many others have left testimonies of the war and of what happened in the concentration camps, but I believe that my voice was able to reach the hearts of many people because I never focused on the horror, but always on HOPE, because *despite everything I believe that people are good at heart.*

Martin Luther King Jr. 1929–1968

I have a dream are the first words of one of my most
famous speeches – the one I gave before a huge crowd of
people that had gathered in front of the Lincoln Memorial
after having PEACEFULLY MARCHED ON WASHINGTON
IN THE NAME OF CIVIL RIGHTS. It was August 28,
1963, and I had been fighting for years to put forward my
DREAM OF A BETTER WORLD, a world in which my
children could live without being considered different only
because of the COLOR OF THEIR SKIN. I always believed
in NONVIOLENCE, and I spent most of my life preaching
my message of hope and faith in the brotherhood of all men.
Counting on the greatest of all super powers, FAITH IN
HUMANKIND, I put myself on the line because
no one is free until we are all free.

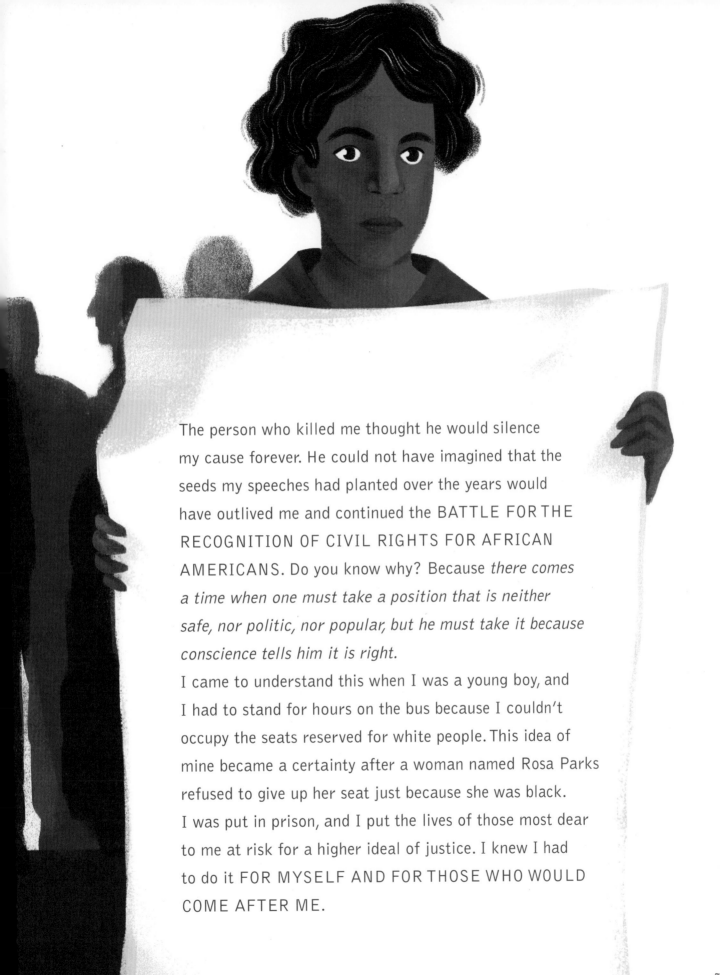

The person who killed me thought he would silence my cause forever. He could not have imagined that the seeds my speeches had planted over the years would have outlived me and continued the BATTLE FOR THE RECOGNITION OF CIVIL RIGHTS FOR AFRICAN AMERICANS. Do you know why? Because *there comes a time when one must take a position that is neither safe, nor politic, nor popular, but he must take it because conscience tells him it is right.*

I came to understand this when I was a young boy, and I had to stand for hours on the bus because I couldn't occupy the seats reserved for white people. This idea of mine became a certainty after a woman named Rosa Parks refused to give up her seat just because she was black. I was put in prison, and I put the lives of those most dear to me at risk for a higher ideal of justice. I knew I had to do it FOR MYSELF AND FOR THOSE WHO WOULD COME AFTER ME.

Neil Armstrong

1930–2012

That's one small step for a man, one giant leap for mankind are the words I pronounced when I set foot on the moon. That day, JULY 20, 1969, left a deep mark in my life as well as in those of my contemporaries and of those who came after me. Until that day, I had been just a man who loved to fly, but then I became a hero who had accomplished a mission that, until then, was believed impossible: TO SET FOOT ON THE MOON, where no human had ever been before. Those were the years of the space race. The Soviets were ahead of us; they had been the first to send a man – cosmonaut Yuri Gagarin – into orbit around Earth. As an American, a man, and a dreamer, I wanted to equal that feat, and thanks to that dream, I had the opportunity to go for a walk on our moon. And do you know what I discovered? To reach your goals you only need one super power: TENACITY.

The first time my feet left the ground, I was only a child: a first flight like many others. But by the time I landed, I knew flying was my destiny. I WANTED TO BE A PILOT, to be in the air admiring the world's beauty from up high. I even fought in the Korean War before I approached the ambitious "MAN IN SPACE SOONEST" program to beat the Soviet Union, the nation that, at the time, was the strongest in space-related projects.

THE APOLLO PROGRAM, particularly when I was CHOSEN AS COMMANDER OF THE *APOLLO 11* mission, marked a turning point in my life. My friends and colleagues Michael Collins and Buzz Aldrin were with me. Together, the three of us conquered the moon, but I had the honor of BEING THE FIRST TO SET FOOT on its surface: an untouched land that others who came after us would also walk on and study.

Dian
Fossey
1932–1985

I always took risks, and I was often misunderstood, but I had to be determined if I wanted to save my gorillas. I CHOSE TO LIVE IN AFRICA, and I chose to study these apes, although, as a matter of fact, I believe it was the gorillas who chose me. I lived so many years with these incredible animals that the locals renamed me "THE WOMAN WHO LIVES ALONE ON THE MOUNTAIN." But I was never alone. I had Digit with me, the male gorilla you see touching my hair in the famous photo, and the other gorillas, too. And then there were the poachers, those I fought against, in every possible way. I fought with all my strength, I was considered an extremist, and I fought to the death. I had to. To protect the gorillas and their habitat, I had to use MY SUPER POWERS, GRIT AND DETERMINATION.

Because of my ideas, I was killed on December 26, 1985. They found my body the following day. Someone killed me with a *panga*, the same weapon they used against my beloved gorillas, against my Digit. I remained in the forest TO DEFEND WITH MY LIFE THE CREATURES I LOVED, because I have always thought that PROTECTING NATURE AND THE ANIMALS IS A WAY OF PROTECTING ALL OF US: *the man who kills animals today is the man who kills people who get in his way tomorrow*. Besides my lifelong study of gorillas, the dedication I put into protecting this species, and my book *Gorillas in the Mist*, which contains a wealth of information on these animals, I also created the Dian Fossey Gorilla Fund for future generations to continue this battle in my place.

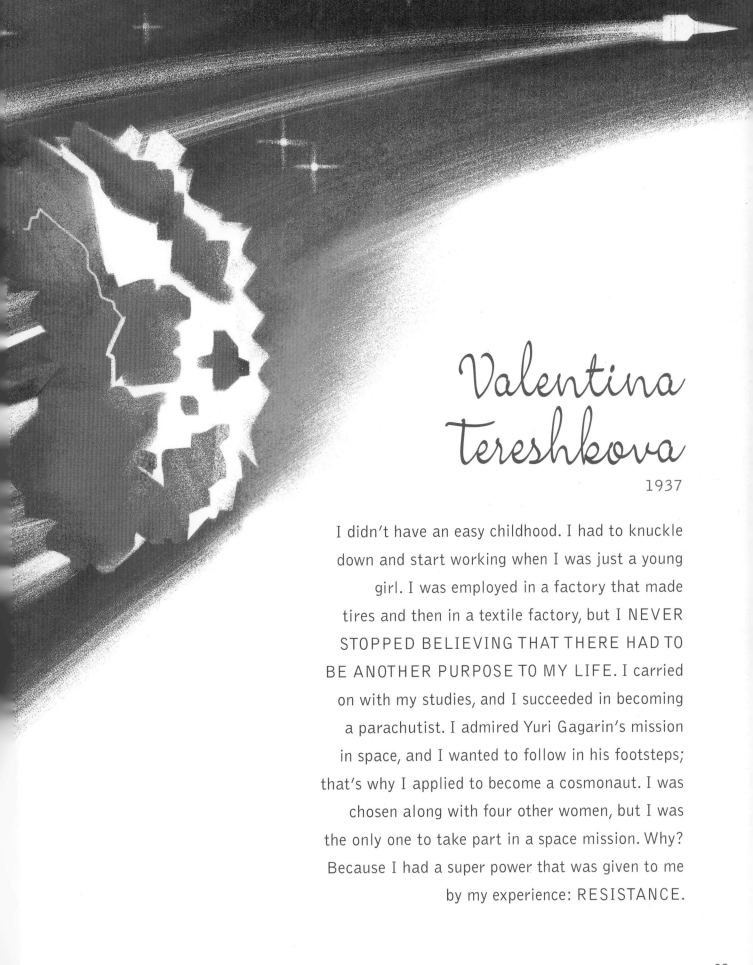

Valentina Tereshkova

1937

I didn't have an easy childhood. I had to knuckle down and start working when I was just a young girl. I was employed in a factory that made tires and then in a textile factory, but I NEVER STOPPED BELIEVING THAT THERE HAD TO BE ANOTHER PURPOSE TO MY LIFE. I carried on with my studies, and I succeeded in becoming a parachutist. I admired Yuri Gagarin's mission in space, and I wanted to follow in his footsteps; that's why I applied to become a cosmonaut. I was chosen along with four other women, but I was the only one to take part in a space mission. Why? Because I had a super power that was given to me by my experience: RESISTANCE.

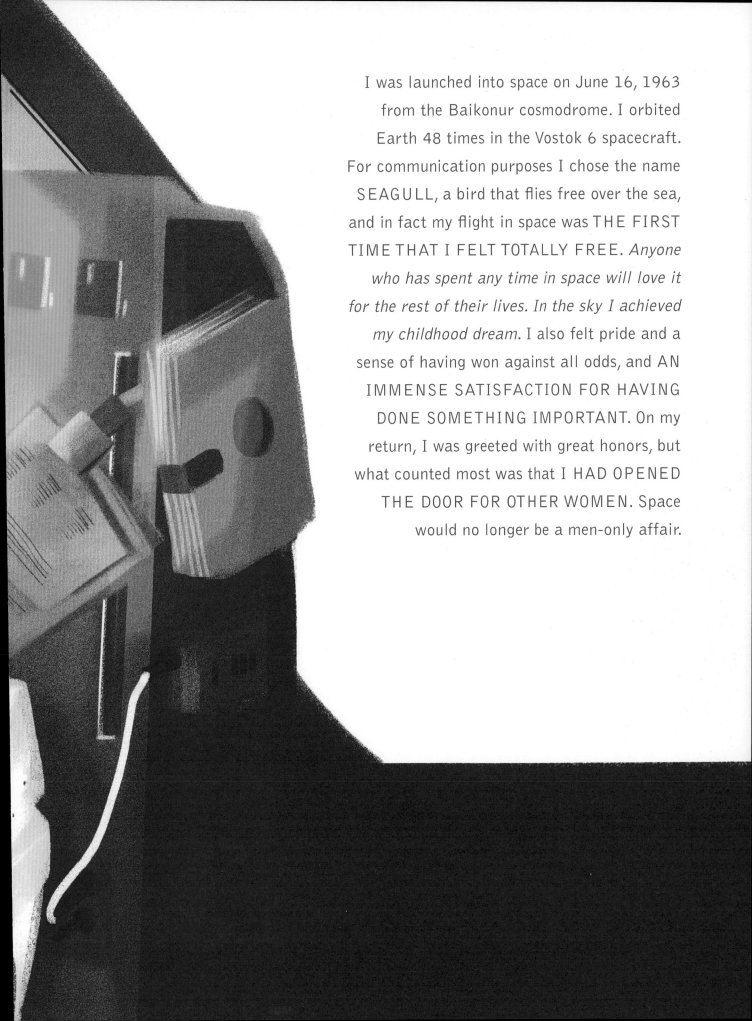

I was launched into space on June 16, 1963 from the Baikonur cosmodrome. I orbited Earth 48 times in the Vostok 6 spacecraft. For communication purposes I chose the name SEAGULL, a bird that flies free over the sea, and in fact my flight in space was THE FIRST TIME THAT I FELT TOTALLY FREE. *Anyone who has spent any time in space will love it for the rest of their lives. In the sky I achieved my childhood dream.* I also felt pride and a sense of having won against all odds, and AN IMMENSE SATISFACTION FOR HAVING DONE SOMETHING IMPORTANT. On my return, I was greeted with great honors, but what counted most was that I HAD OPENED THE DOOR FOR OTHER WOMEN. Space would no longer be a men-only affair.

Stephen Hawking 1942–2018

For most of my life, I was the PRISONER OF MY BODY. Like an oyster inside its shell. Yet I never for one second stopped thinking and speculating, and this allowed me to yield a number of pearls: several scientific theories that have advanced OUR KNOWLEDGE OF THE UNIVERSE. In 1963, when I was an eager student at Cambridge, I was diagnosed with a degenerative disease. I was told I had only two years left to live. But I reached the age of 76. I married, I had children and grandchildren, but most important, I MADE GREAT DISCOVERIES, like the radiation that was named after me: the Hawking radiation. How did I do it? With MY SUPER POWER: FAITH IN REASON!

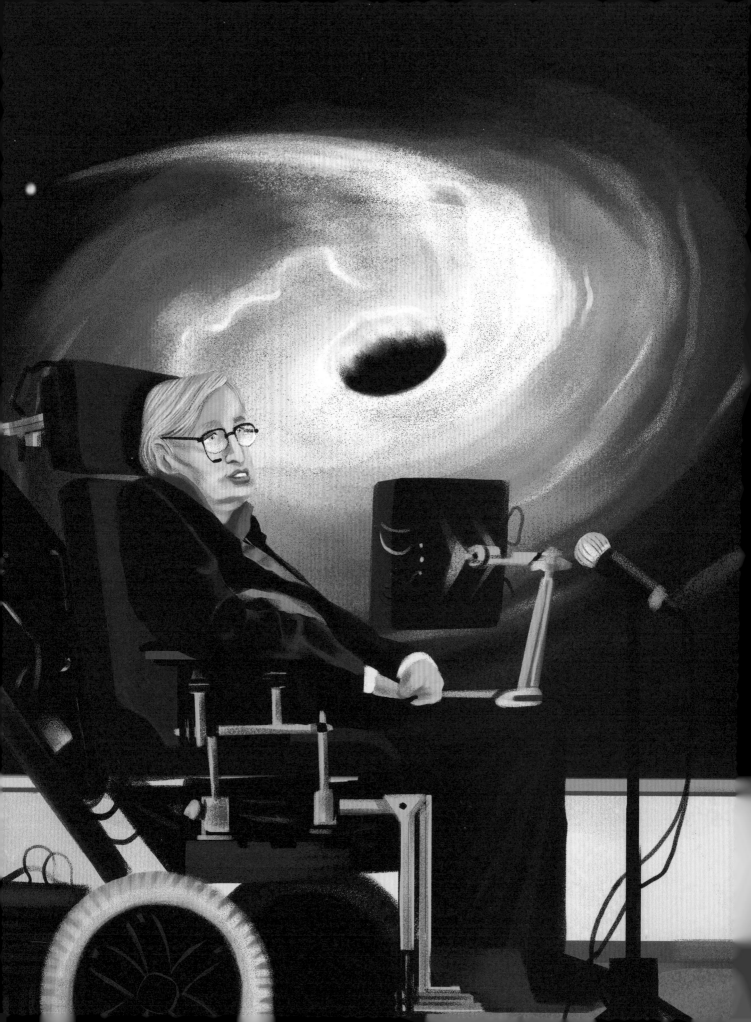

However difficult life may seem, there is always something you can do. Remember to look up at the stars and not down at your feet. This has been my motto throughout my whole life. When I thought that there was nothing else for me to do, I USED TO SPEND MY TIME STARING UP AT THE SKY! But then I took control of my life and made a masterpiece out of it. I STUDIED THE MYSTERY OF BLACK HOLES, I tried to discover THE ORIGIN OF TIME, I studied THE POSSIBLE ALTERNATIVE THEORIES ON THE COSMOS, and I worked to make my theories known. I held lectures all over the world, I wrote books, and I took part in TV programs. I believed science should be accessible to everyone, comprehensible, and capable of triggering action. Sitting on my wheel chair, with a speech synthesizer to voice my thoughts, I found sense in what did not have any sense, because *when one's expectations are reduced to zero, one really appreciates everything one does have.*

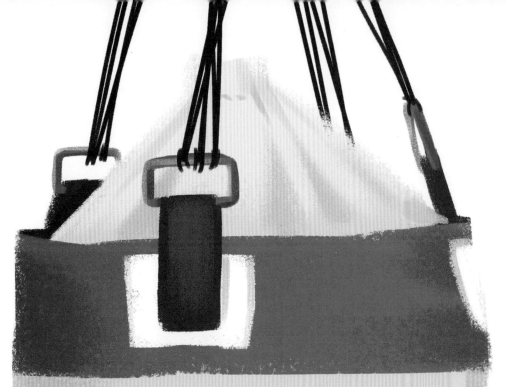

Muhammad Ali

1942–2016

I am known AS THE GREATEST BOXER OF ALL TIME, but I was much more than that. I showed a new way of living to those like me, who risked using violence, and to all those young boys lost in the streets with no dreams or hopes. I was Cassius Clay, a kid, a man, who climbed into the ring TO CHANNEL HIS ANGER into a fair, clean fight by pulling punches in a boxing match. Later I became Muhammad Ali, the hero for my people, the African Americans, in a country — America — that was still deeply stricken by racial hatred. Ever since I was a small boy, I realized I had a super power that could be dangerous, a kind of strength that can lean toward anger, but I decided that my super power would become my ally for doing good things. One day I was told: "Climb into the ring!" Nothing was ever the same.

I lost count of how many times I was named "boxer of the year." I won a gold medal at the Olympic Games, I was a heavyweight champion several times, and I beat countless opponents with knockouts that have gone down in history, but the challenge of which I am most proud IS CARRYING THE OLYMPIC TORCH at the Atlanta Olympics in 1996. I was suffering from Parkinson's disease, but I managed to light the Olympic brazier even though my hand was trembling and my feet moved with difficulty.

By tackling my illness, I showed the same
determination that made me a great boxer
and worthy of the Presidential Medal of
Freedom. I showed everyone that strength
can lead to something good, but only if it
is used RESPECTING AND HELPING
THOSE AROUND US.

Bobbi Gibb 1942

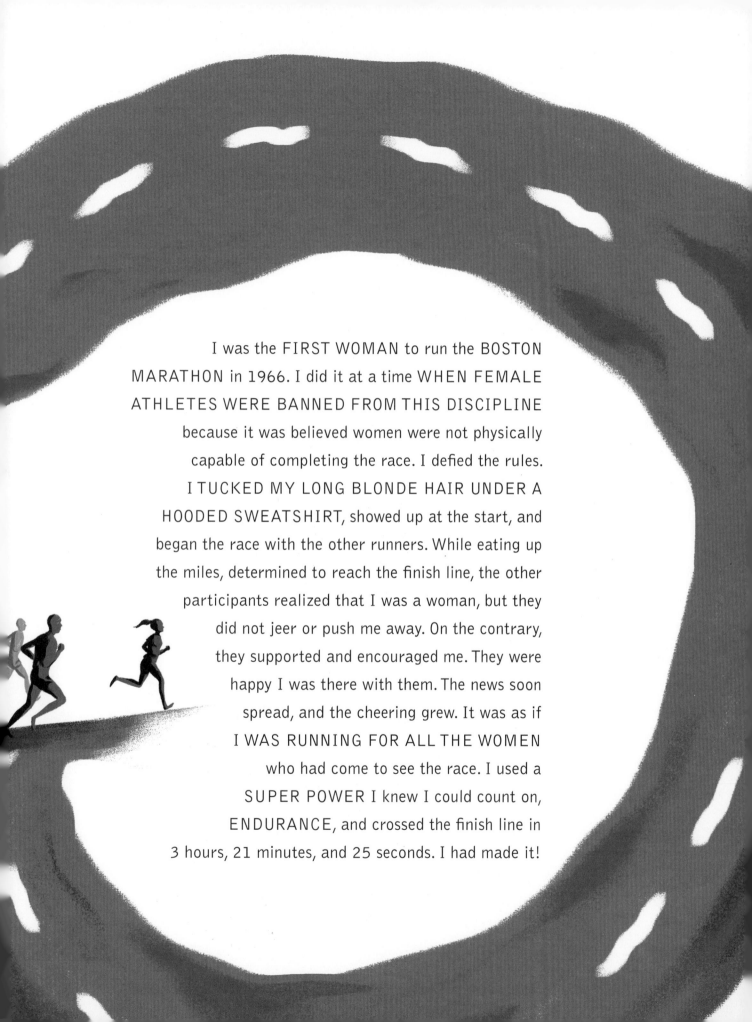

I was the FIRST WOMAN to run the BOSTON MARATHON in 1966. I did it at a time WHEN FEMALE ATHLETES WERE BANNED FROM THIS DISCIPLINE because it was believed women were not physically capable of completing the race. I defied the rules. I TUCKED MY LONG BLONDE HAIR UNDER A HOODED SWEATSHIRT, showed up at the start, and began the race with the other runners. While eating up the miles, determined to reach the finish line, the other participants realized that I was a woman, but they did not jeer or push me away. On the contrary, they supported and encouraged me. They were happy I was there with them. The news soon spread, and the cheering grew. It was as if I WAS RUNNING FOR ALL THE WOMEN who had come to see the race. I used a SUPER POWER I knew I could count on, ENDURANCE, and crossed the finish line in 3 hours, 21 minutes, and 25 seconds. I had made it!

I thought how many preconceived prejudices would crumble when I trotted right along for twenty-six miles! I have run all my life, and I love it. When I grew up, I was determined to participate in a prestigious competition like the Boston Marathon. When I WAS TOLD I COULD NOT, JUST BECAUSE I WAS A WOMAN, I could not accept it. I felt I had to put things straight. It was no longer only about running, it was about proving that I could run a marathon even if I was a woman, and THAT EVERY WOMAN COULD DO IT, IF SHE SET HER MIND TO IT. I thought of how many wrong ideas one can have, of how many preconceptions can stop people from making their dreams come true. When I decided to join the race as an unauthorized participant, I did it for every man and woman's right to decide their destiny, regardless of gender, social status, or cultural origin. *I ran the Boston Marathon out of love. [...] Yet it was a love that was incomplete until it was shared with others.*

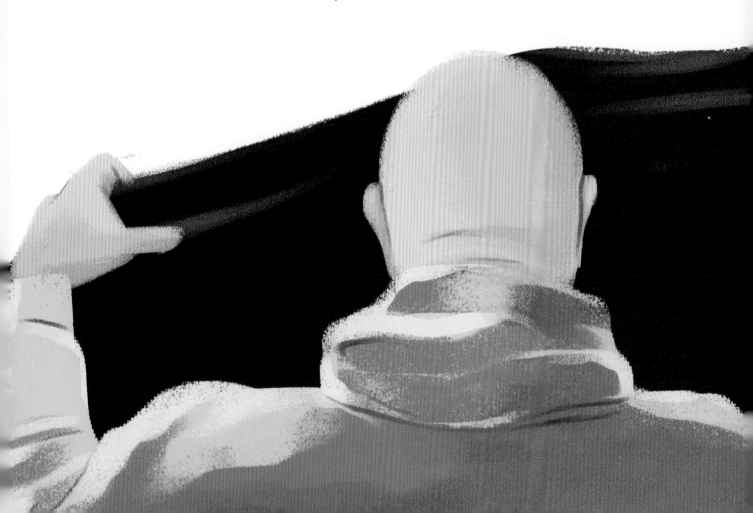

Malala Yousafzai 1997

I never wanted to
become a hero. All I
cared for was studying.
I used to live in a
village in the Swat Valley
in Pakistan. My life was happy.
I had lots of friends, a loving family, and
BOOKS TO HELP ME DREAM about my
future. But when I turned eleven, things changed
dramatically. The Taliban arrived, and they started
closing down schools, stopping girls from going to class,
and making up laws that limited people's freedom. I
started WRITING A BLOG to claim those rights that
somebody wanted to take away from me and my people.
I was punished for this. They tried to silence me, to
break my spirit, but they failed. They did not know I had
a super power that made me stronger than them: my
LOVE of truth, liberty, and equality, which is greater
than their love of hatred.

On October 9, 2012, my life changed, forever. Some men who opposed my commitment to women's education got on the bus I was traveling on and shot me in the head. I was only fifteen years old. I FOUGHT TO SURVIVE. For a long time my condition was very uncertain; nobody knew if I would ever recover. They thought they would break me, but I was stronger than them. I felt I had a goal in life that was bigger than myself, and I fought as hard as I could to reach it. I wrote a book, I was awarded the Nobel Peace Prize, and I have created the Malala Fund to support girls' rights to go to school. But my job is not over yet. It won't be UNTIL EVERY WOMAN IS FREE TO CHOOSE HER DESTINY, just as I did. I deeply believe in what I often repeat: *one child, one teacher, one book, one pen can change the world*. I am trying to make this happen.

Afterword

After reading about the incredible events in the lives of these SUPERHEROES WHO LIVED WITHOUT MASKS AND WITHOUT FEAR, are you still convinced that extraordinary powers are needed to save the world? COURAGE, DETERMINATION, AND TALENT are only some of the qualities used by these men and women to change society. They fought to ASSERT THEIR IDEAS, to DEFEND THE RIGHTS OF OTHERS, and to BETTER THE WORLD, and they never gave up.

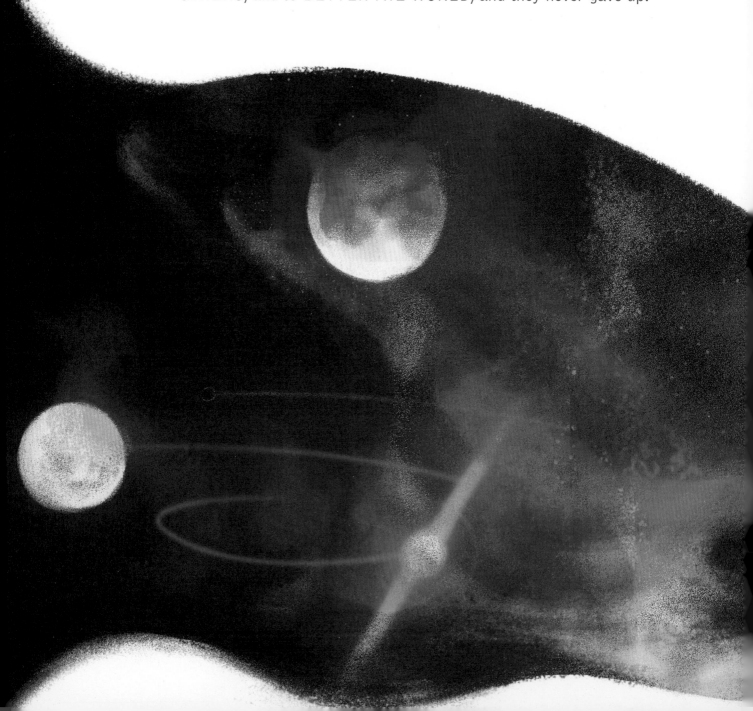

They experienced DRAMATIC MOMENTS, they gave up a lot, sometimes even their lives, and they resisted WITHOUT EVER GIVING IN TO DISCOURAGEMENT. In the end they left an indelible sign of their presence — and a warning — that we should follow their example. After all, THE EARTH STILL NEEDS SUPERHEROES, especially those armed with pens, a voice, intelligence, intuition, and perseverance.

THEY NEED YOU, your INCREDIBLE TALENTS, and YOUR GENEROUS HEART.

After having shared this exciting journey with so many real superheroes, WOULDN'T YOU LIKE TO BE ONE OF THEM, TOO? Perhaps you don't think you have any particular powers, but TRY LOOKING AT YOURSELF IN THE MIRROR and you'll immediately see the reflection of EVERYTHING YOU NEED! Inside you there is already that something that makes you UNIQUE AND INCREDIBLY STRONG. All you must do is take YOUR SECRET POWER, add a pinch of COURAGE, plenty of DETERMINATION, and a lot of IMAGINATION, and you will be ready to FOLLOW YOUR DREAMS wherever they may take you!